BAZ UBER ALLES

The Complete Baz Poems

Kevin Cadwallender

dogeater
books that bite

First Published in the UK in 2004 by Dogeater
PO Box 990 Newcastle upon Tyne NE99 2US
www.dogeater.co.uk

Typeset in Garamond

Cover design and typesetting by Dogeater

'Baz tattoo' courtesy of Eddie Hardiman
Eddie's Tattoo Studio
121 Third Street
Horden, Peterlee
Co. Durham SR8 4EH

Printed in the UK by Biddles Ltd

ISBN 0 9546515 0 2

‘Every Baz I will go with you
And you will be my guide’

Contents

Baz Nativity

A virgin birth
on Boxing Day,
Christ knew where the father was.
Baz was born bloody
and cursed,

the umbilical cord
twisted about his neck,
blue with cold rage
and daring
God to take him…

if he were hard enough.

Magi backing away
not wanting any trouble.

Baz Loco Parentis

Without a Dad
Baz should have become
softer, swathed by
his mother's feminine
instinct.

She lit a match
and with a roll of *Drum*
smoked an
excuse to leave him
with neighbours.

Baz told me later
of all his Dads
only his birthfather
had the guts to desert him
without hurting him.

His Mother kindled
his skill at survival,
lit his first cigarette,
cast him into Gehen'na.

She had a profound effect on his life,
he could not speak about her
without kicking you unconscious.

Baz the Younger Goes to War

Lining up soldiers
behind lego barricades
in Baz's Mam's bathroom,
we would recreate
unspecified carnage
with an aerial bombardment
of glass alleys,
both sides countenancing
massive losses without
hope of armistice.

One remembrance Sunday
with a steel ball bearing
as big as a tennis ball,
Baz brought the ultimate
deterrent to bear.
And with the shattering of
plastic buildings
and plastic men
came the sickening
crack of bone.

In hospital
Baz marvelled
at the resilience
of flesh,
accepting the
white face of
my surrender
with gracious ease.

Baz Inherits a Dad

When Baz's Mam got married
Baz got a Dad,
I remember his tears
burns cut his mucky cheeks,
the first time he was strapped.

He showed me the welts
of skin underneath his jumper,
I told him my sister had headlice
to cheer him up.

We went to point at her
as she wailed under the fine-tooth comb.

He said,
'It's great Kev,
I've never had a Dad
who beats you like a Dad should'

I lay awake thinking about those words
but couldn't grasp the logic.

My head itched through thinking too much.

Baz Wept

An empty rabbit hutch
and the smell of baking
brought home the transience
of life and the foolishness
of getting involved.

Still, Baz and me
buried the pie in
a next door
neighbour's garden.

Fingerprints in flour
and soil beneath our nails
giving us away to our
fathers' leather belts.

Yet it was worth
the pain, striking
a final blow for innocence.

Julian and Baz

Paired in English,
like the first meeting
of Cro-magnon and Neanderthal,
uncomprehending,
incapable of anything
that might connect.

They share primitive
hand gestures, facial grins
Baz assaults the paper
with his pen.

Baz offers Julian a 'polo.'
Julian invents the wheel.

Baz Pisces

Sticklebacks and frogspawn
dead in a cracked fishtank
in the back of his new Dad's shed,
Stinking their way out
into a Spring twilight.

For Baz's Dad
a leather strap
eliminated the need
for debate.

Baz never flinched though
and spat out blood where
he'd bit through his lip.
When his Dad died
Baz cried all day.

Baz's uncle won him
a goldfish at the shows
and bought him
a bowl
and everything.

Baz said,
'He's not my real Uncle.'

Baz Lex Talio Nis

Bullied once too often
in the juniors
and dreading the
final bell.

On that long march home
not daring to look back,
leering voices scuffling
at my haversack straps.

Yells and commotion
cry-baby calls
mocking my misery
and coward's yellow
colouring my guts.
Turning to face
my demons
and seeing Baz
dervishing his
towel bag into
the enemy ranks,
I charged too
and we routed
them all.

Baz grinning like a maniac
at my mute appreciation,
escorted me to my house
saluted and sounded the all clear.

Stopping only once
To empty the brick from his towel bag.

Kenny and the Art of Pugilism

Got some boxing gloves one Christmas
and a punch ball, red leather,
knocked hell out of it, it never hit back.
Me and Kenny, one afternoon
had a boxing match, same present see.
We sparred and lightly tapped each other,
he jabbed me once or twice, nicked my cheek
with rough sewn seams.
We floated like butterflies for a bit
although my style was a bit more moth bitten
and then he stung me like a bastard bee
and opened up a lightning gash
under my left eye, with a hammered-home fist,
full-force and followed up expertly
with a lethal combination that
left my nose spread across my face
all blood and snot.
I went fucking light and pummelled him
with outrageous roundhouses
with him saying sorry and
putting his guard up to fend me off.
A sort of cross between *Raging Bull*
and Tommy Steele's *Little White Bull.*
I flailed until he pinned me
with a left hook that put me down
and counting backwards in frustration.

I swapped my gloves for a subbuteo

Kenny got put in borstal for knifing his Dad.

Julian and the Orbilian Stick

In the library surrounded by lies
books full of them;
lies about love and
lies about poetry,
Julian swallows enough
to make every day a summer.

Imagination turning him inside out,
when the other boys were dull and flat.

We caned him every day with ignorance.

Baz and Billy and Kenny and me

An unholy trinity
joined at birth
by circumstance
and class.
Baz says,
'We're like the three musketeers'
and I suppose I don't mind
being D'artagnan to his Porthos.

We sit around a beach campfire
watching moths flicker in smoke.
Baz throws me a can of cooking lager
and says in a moment of clarity.

'Y'know Kevin I don't know why you bother with a
bunch of losers like us'

I protest his deprecating definition
accompanied by the hoots and howls
of Kenny and Billy who have
never had cause to wonder much.

Baz opens a Guinness with a flourish
sups the cream like a pup at a teat
grinning with his foam moustache
in the orange firelight where
Carter topped the bloke on the aerial flights.

'All for one and one for all' he rallies
raising aluminium ring pulls to the heavens
Our imagined steel cuts the night
Binds us together in dark blood.

Baz, Biology and the Lash

(no hamsters were harmed in the making of this poem)

Bored to 'O' level
in the Biology lab,
confronted by XX and XY
and a teacher keen
on sexual equations,

Baz at a loss
for answers gassed
the school hamster
with a blown out
bunsen burner.

'What kind of a moron are you?'
asked Mr.Chapman.

It was the first time I ever saw a teacher bleed.

Mr. Harrison it seems
used to be an amateur boxer
before he became a lab technician.

Baz says
that corporal punishment
is a waste of time and
he should know
his brother was
once birched
on a day trip
to the
Isle of Man.

Baz in the Perfumed Garden

School sportsday
in the 1500 metres
Baz once stopped
to chat up a lass
from the Catholic school.
He came last
and got six
on each hand
but he reckoned
it was worth it.

Later and with
a lovebite *in situ*
he charged us 20 pence
to smell his middle finger.

Baz and the Word

Baz's theory is that the word 'fuck'
if used enough, will negate itself,
he doesn't say it in those words
but his use of the expletive is profound
and borderline fanatical.

History proves this he tells me
although he doesn't specify which bit
or locate his philosophy exactly.
He puts his hand in his jeans
and puts copper in the Salvation Army
collection tin, collaring the poor sod
for Baz's anniversary sermon.

In the beginning Baz says
the Earth was without form and that,
and desolate -ish
and God or 'fucking' God
didn't give a fuck
so he gave us religion, oh and er... water
and swearing which is like blasphemy.
Baz the Baptist pauses for an epiphany,
God gave us the word fuck
he finally blurts out,
a revelation at his mind's edge.
It is our birthright
fuck is god fucking given
fucking hell!
fuck means fuck all.
The Smirnoff at this point
has reached his brain.
He falls backwards

taking out a table
of drinks.
The Young Soldier of Christ
makes a run for it, sensibly.
We see his banners fly.

Maybe Baz is right.
Linguists gather at his feet.
Maybe Baz just likes to say the word.
Maybe Baz really gives a fuck.
I pick him up with Kenny at his other arm

'In the beginning was the word'
he says,
like a universe collapsing in on itself
without a big bang.

The Building Trade

Julian is an existentialist. He works on a building site
with Tom the labourer, Fred the brickie and Bob the hod carrier.
It works like this: Tom fills Bob's hod up with bricks,
Bob carries them to Fred and Fred builds a wall.
Julian's job is to help the bricks understand their own reality.

Tom has ham sandwiches for lunch,
Bob has cheese and Fred has egg.
Julian doesn't have lunch as he feels this is saying 'no'
to a society which insists on social imperatives such as lunch.

Sometimes the bricks argue with Julian saying
'But we have the right to freedom.'
Julian smiles, 'Man is condemned to freedom.'
'But we are bricks' they cry, 'why do you oppress us?'
Some days the walls just don't get built at all.
Julian doesn't sleep well.
He dreams of a mass uprising of bricks,
of boundaries collapsing all over suburbia,
of Sunday morning street warfare with flymos
and hovers clashing over disputed inches of turf,
of middle-class landowners with nothing to keep
their mortgages in. . .
secretly,

Tom practises hod carrying
Bob practises bricklaying
and Fred is doing a night class in sociology.
Julian is an existentialist and lives outside
of the restrictions placed upon him by the
constant problem of having no self to esteem
and no self to be 'ish' with.

This however does not prevent his sleeping
with the gaffer's daughter who has
a Btec in Freudian hairdressing,
which means that everytime
she cuts someone's hair
they look like a dick.

The French Connection

Here Kev, you do writing
write us a poem
will yer?
To Julie
she sez she'll
giz it if yer can.

Din't use nee
big words mind
and nowt too puffy
just enough to, yer knaa,
get me end away.

How... it's just like
that police bloke
from Jersey in France,
innit,
yer knaa
Bergerac.

Cyrano de Bergerac.

Kenny Goes Fly Fishing

Kenny is necking on with Debbie
in the phone box outside of the
delicatessen that used to be the butchers.
It's Kenny's favourite spot for romance
it's the place he took Tracy and Sharon.
Kenny knows all the jokes
you can make in a phone box,
he has rehearsed each pun about 'chat up lines'
every double entendre about
trunk calls and handling his receiver.
Debbie thinks that Kenny is dead funny,
she laughs a bit like Tracy
but not as much as Sharon.

Kenny knows when to drop in the coins,
when to let his fingers do the talking,
Kenny knows just the moment to
slip his hand inside her blouse.

Debbie slapped Kenny hard
but not as hard as Tracy
or as passionately as Sharon.
Kenny's getting better at this;
he's got their numbers
although
he's just tossing
in a phonebox
when it comes to
cracking their codes.

Billy, the Illustrated Man

Billy's got a tattoo
it runs the length of his arm
it is a record of conquests
real and imagined.
It remembers every woman
with a notch in the form
of a blue-blank slotted
between every red and green
coil of every snake.
The needle has ran him seam to seam
blood and ink, his diary illustrated on his body.

'What'll you do when you run out of skin?'
asks one of the more concerned punters.
'What'll I do when I run out of women,
more likely' he quips.

But the ink is clouding his judgement
the writing isn't only on the wall,
he is crushed, breathless by fortune's coils
as the arm bunches together to throw a dart
and flexes into blurred sky.
They are building new estates
where he was brought up
encroaching on the homelands.

'Cut here' at his wrist.

'Mam' shrined in a daggered heart.

Julie and Debbie and Tracy and Sharon

Teetering on stilettos
and alco-pops to
the *Tuxedo Princess,*
Debbie chucks up
over Gateshead,
in the shadow of
Culture,
while Sharon
gets a love bite
from her
sister's husband.
Tracy has borrowed the car keys
and gone to fuck
a bass player.

Meanwhile Julie
in pensive mood
and being the
designated driver
lights a cigarette end
on the quiet Tyne
remembers bridges
are built to connect,
thinks about doing
a night-class in typing.

Smoke is whisked away
to exotic Newcastle,
Brendan's Benidorm
over the Millennium eye
a bow shot away.

Julian and The Final Frontier

Julian is a Klingon *Bird of Prey* pilot,
he studies I.T. at the university,
he speaks several languages,
all of them are from Star Trek.

In the summer he signs on
citing as his preferred occupation
'Pilot, cloaked or uncloaked'.
The D.S.S. supervisor has bought
an English/Klingon dictionary
she is learning how to say
'suspended from benefits'
but for now she leans
across the counter and says,
'Do KHA' which means
'that is unfortunate.'

Julian duly amends his form
To 'anything in computers'
(Borg and Cardassian empires excluded).
How far he is willing to travel
depends on the warp capacity
of his 'wessell'
a clapped out Ford Fiesta
bought via the internet from
the Ferrenghi chemistry student
at Manchester University.

Julian got a job at McDonalds
where he is an extra, waiting
to be beamed off the planet's surface.
Uses his expertise to teach the customer service droids

the perfect Vulcan death grip,
taught to him in secret by Sheila the
T'pau lookalike who cleans the humans'
lavatories.

Baz And the Freedom of the Press

Full of Hell
Baz gatecrashes the chip shop,
bringing down on the counter a greasy
newspaper, bearing a colour image
of a topless model.

'It's a fucking disgrace, you should
watch what you're selling,
I bought them chips for my little girl!'

The chip shop owner is
caught somewhere between
bemused and terrified and
pours two lots of vinegar
on some wifie's tail-end.

He stutters meekly
'But... but... I only sell chips!'

Baz rumbles on about guards in Auschwitz
and then explodes,
'Bloody typical,
I bet you're a Tory,
only a bloody Tory rag
would print this filth
and only a Tory would
wrap up a little girl's chips
in pornography.'

'But… but…'
The chip shop queue
have formed a moral majority,
nodding their outrage

and checking their
wrappings for nudes.

The poor bastard is sweating now
and apologizing, he offers Baz
a free fish and chip lunch.
Baz graciously accepts the offer.
The queue warmly applauds his exit.

Outside I remind Baz
that he hasn't got a little girl
and he reminds me
who's got the free lunch.

Baz Psycho

See that film
was all wrong,
He would've shagged her
before he killed her, man.
Janet Leigh?
Wouldn't you?
Well I would anyroads.

And he should never
have kept them bodies
in that freezer,
they'd only keep
for three month, tops.
He should've gone to B&Q
and bought one of them cheap
circular saws, cut them
into little pieces and left
them out for the birds.
Daphne Du Maurier eh?
What's she got to do with it.
Small chunks big enough
for spuggies to take.
Well that's what I'd do
anyroads.

You see that knife
there's no way he
would have held it
like that, leaves his guts
exposed man,

he should've held it like this.
What if there'd been
a dozen hairy bikers in that shower?
What?
Twelve Angry Men?
Maybe. I dunno

It's common sense.
Well that's all I'm sayin'
anyroads.

Julian and the Occult

Julian is a Witchfinder General.
He works at *Pets 'R' Us*,
stalking all the demons
who talk to cats and
buy their familiars gifts.

Cutting a swathe in his Hopkins hat.
A birch rod swishing through the aisles.

At night he interrogates
the mute snakes,
the evil hamsters, wet
from his miniature ducking stool.
Scoops the floating fish
from the hubble bubble of tanks,
proclaims them innocent.

Once he told me,
over non-alcoholic lager,
that he'd seen the great Satan
shopping for souls in Sainsburys,
where Julian has a part time job
stacking shelves on the nightshift.

'When do you find time to sleep'
I ask him.
He looks at me like I've masturbated in church.
A cruel sneer twisting his lips,
crying with a voice
from purgatory,

'Sleep! Sleep!
Evil never sleeps,
Evil never sleeps.'

Tracy's True Colours

Tracy has two babies,
one black, one white,
calls them her own private 'toon army',
takes them to sit in the stands.
One of them was once kissed by Kevin Keegan
on a day when the press were invited.
Tracy spends her child benefit
on season tickets and 'babygros',
breast feeds behind the opposition goal,
has a tattoo on her wrist of a magpie,
collects autographs like silver paper,
precious little names glued
on the walls of her nest.
Waiting for the landlord to come
and fix the gas fire,
decided her kids would be
better off in the care
of rugby union supporters.
Left a scribbled note;
black biro on white and
two kids wrapped in
a hand knitted scarf
in away colours.

Sharon's Choice

'So I took him off the cow
and she sodded off somewhere
I even got her house
he said she was rubbish in bed
I never liked her much anyway
it's not like we were close
a stuck up bitch
no there was no children involved
we were never friends just sisters.'

In retrospect her sister's husband
might not have been the catch of the century,
three kids down the line, he is out at the pub,
she is at home watching Coronation Street
while her sister changed her life;
went to university, bagged a professor
got a big house in Northumberland somewhere.

'She took my husband the cow
I let her have the house
I just felt sick
he was inadequate in bed
she never liked me anyway
I had ideas above my station
she used to say it to him
I have two children now
one of each, we were sisters,
we don't speak, never will.
In retrospect she did me a favour
I wouldn't change what I've got now,
she took what she wanted
I hope she got what she expected.'

'If she were alive today
My mother would be spinning in her grave.'

Baz at Stamford Bridge

Drunk and disorderly
in the overnight cell,
Baz nurses his bruises
after an away defeat
at Chelsea.
Happy as a scarf
on a terrace
Baz beams,

'Cheaper than bed and breakfast, man!'

And I know he's right
but my ribs are sore
and I've started to
look forward to
winter
and the weeks
when the
pools panel sits.

Baz and the Fascists

When Baz stopped bedwetting
and invited us up to the musty
miasma of his secret passions

It was like 'Joplings' window gone mad;
mannequins kitted out in Nazi regalia,
a primitive arsenal of death stars,
crossbows and rice-flails.
Like part of his childhood
got fucked up by the bastard brood
of Bruce Lee and Eva Braun.

One day pissed in Sunderland High Street,
confronted by some National Front skin
with a copy of 'Bulldog' waving like a flag,
Baz took off his 'dut' and with
rhino-like accuracy
head butted him to the ground

and it was poppy day all over the place.

'That's for me Granddad,' Baz muttered
moving off in search of new lethal weapons.

Baz and the Intentional Fallacy

Baz bruises easy
lovebites like gobstoppers
pearling his neck.
Grinning like he
ate a Cheshire cat
and I know we're
gonna get the whole
grisly affair with
sordid colour supplements
for the next fortnight
and innuendo and out again
and marks out of ten
and the rake's progress
and nobody, but nobody
will dare to suggest
what we're all thinking
as he struts like a bellicose
bantam to the bar at last.

'Cos Baz is hard.
I know, he sez so
and so do his tattoos
and as he always says
before he drops you,

'On the one hand there's L.O.V.E

and on the other there is….

Baz Cher Chez La Femme

Baz has an idea,
first one this decade.
Let's go to Blackpool
do the lights,
do Yates' Wine Lodge
howk up from the
top of the tower,
buy paintstripper grade
vodka from the off door.

Drinking himself senseless
in senselessly expensive bedsits
Baz pisses the bed drunk
smuggles out sodden sheets and pillows
after a hasty, greasy breakfast
dumps the lot in a bottle bank.

At the disco
Baz smooth as diarrhoea
sidles up to his intended
a grope itching in his groin

'Do yer wanna dance?'
he says, cool as anti-freeze.

'I already am'
She smiles sweet as an assassin.

Minutes of rehearsed
sophistication are
shot to buggery
as he opens his gob.

'Go fuck yourself then!'

Baz lurches back to the bar
orders something poisonous
to keep the lava from boiling over,
leaves the dancefloor
to more sensitive souls.

Baz Goes Dutch

Double Dutch
in Holland,
Baz grasps
the fact that
his vocabulary
does not extend
beyond its
northern confines.
Gazes out of
the coach window
at dutch swans in
dutch canals
muttering,

'Look at all these fuckin' fjords!'

Baz Appreciates Art

Half cut and looking for the final cut,
in a Hamburg *cunsthalle*
with crude jokes and
Baz looking for the bog
that Rodin pissed in.
Insights as profound
as blurb on beermats
bubble out;

'I always liked the *Mona Lisa* mesel',
I read in *Viz* once she had a canny arse.'

Meanwhile in an alternate world
Da Vinci paints *The Tart with the Fat Backside*
as drunks peruse and yearn
for that uncanny smile.

Baz Virgo Nil Intactus

Ten pints of brown ale
and she not far behind
down the back of the
Workies' club
with the urine on bricks
and stale cigarettes
he loses it
after a couple of sly grunts
and her tights
unceremoniously wrinkled
about her ankle chain.
The dull thud of *The Birdy Song*
a rhapsody followed by
a solo
kiss
before the fumble
for words.

And if either one remembers
it'll be a miracle or because
she forgot her pill
like he forgot to
ask her name.

Baz Interferes with the Means of Production

Having had one too many
at the Eyesenck Oyster Bar,
Baz in furtive mood
smooches to Marx
in the flickering T.V. light.
Wet dreams his way
through Rosa and several other
revolutionary role models
before his appetite is
sated like Stalinism
in a curry sauce of anarchy.
Kripotkin and Bakunin
dance without leading
into images of young men
in classrooms of class
where Durkheim was found
beaten into a state of anomie
which led to erotic haiku
and sticky hands
interfering
with various means
of production.

And the posters were mute
Che and Vlad hiding in
incomprehensible
iconography.

Baz Tardy

Some twelve or
fourteen moonshines
lag of a brother.
Baz can still drink
most legitimate boozers
under the formica.

And in the plague of
Customs and Excise
Baz would never permit
the curiosity of nations
or their representatives
to deprive him of booty,
when the dimensions
of a suitcase are as well
compacted with
cigarettes for Mam
and rum for Uncle Bob
as a souvenir
donkey.

Clinking through customs
brazen as necessity,
with gods standing
up and cheering
for bastards.

Baz and the Black Rabbit

and although he never acknowledged
the face behind him in the mirror
the soft coney eyes and twitching nose
it was always there.

in peripheral vision
not daring to look at his wife
in the shadow drawn night.

in dreams, a cloak of skulls,
rows of incisors like claw hammers

all the violence in him
cowering.

Baz and the Bourgeoisie

In her lounge, like she didn't have a living room
and Baz rattling on about how he never scabbed
and me feeling guilty for not being a miner
and the cut glass crystal decanter getting
more and more offensive
and the brass pit lamps were
just as stuck up as her gobshite
of a husband who droned on and on
about his shares in British Gas
and how his *Procol Harum* L.P.'s
were so bastard rare that it didn't matter
if they were crap or not.

And me being polite as usual
and nodding in all the right places
and Baz wanking the West Highland White
under the table with his Major Dommo's
and me bolting Mousakka and
Bull's Blood and trying not to
look down the low cut dress of our
gracious hostess,
who says she and her significant other
have an 'open relationship' from the
'Open University' and I'm thinking,
'I want home' and Baz reckons he's scored
and comes up grinning from under
the table like some perverse
synchronised swimmer.

And I can't find my car keys
and 'significant Gerard' is showing me
his airfix kits and trying to put his hands on me arse
and Baz I can tell is shagging noisily

like a bollock in a china shop,
the Austrian decanter giggles nervously
on the mantelpiece.

And I'm out of there
Baz trailing, cursing, swearing.
falling over his libido
as it pulls it kecks up.

Halfway home he eyes me suspiciously,
'You're a bit of a snob aren't you Kev?'

and reluctantly I have to agree.

Baz and the Ram Raiders

So anyway I'll tell you how it is!
We hot wired this Escort,
no rubbish mind we only twoc G.T's
took it thru the town,
ram raided the job centre
not a job on the premises.
Came out with half a dozen
government schemes and
some crap tapes of lift music.
Can't get rid of the schemes
know how the government feels now,
sold the tapes to me Granny,
she's over the moon thinks it's James Last.

Got nicked last week
driving with no insurance,
no tax, no M.O.T. and… no car.
Bastard surrealist coppers.

So anyway she sez you are a sexist pig
yer never take me anywhere, sez she's
not gonna see me again unless I change,
got some new kegs, new dut and had me
eyebrow pierced, can't say I haven't tried.

Tell yer what to do to stop them petrol bombs
put the price of petrol up!
Didn't see half the violence durin' the gulf war.

How man, yer've seen nowt like it.
It was bliddy great man, hundreds of us
Nah, thousands, rampagin' ower the Tyne Bridge.
It was like a revolution man
in chicken suits and nike shorts.
Aye, a do the Great North Run every year

It keeps us off the streets.

Baz Buys British

Fixing the car
one sedentary Sunday
I hear Baz's air horn
as it blasphemes
at the neighbours.

Baz eyes my
D reg VW Polo
winds down his window
and tuts disapprovingly.

'Y'know y'should really buy British!'
he recites like a tabloid reader.

And finding first gear
with some difficulty
rattles off
back to the smog
in his clapped out
Ford Cortina.

Deborah Rah Rah Rah

When Debbie became Deborah,
traded in the low life for the high,
the girls that weren't invited to
her wedding stood
on the quayside and cried.

To wed a pop star is unlikely;
to wed one of such magnitude
deserved applause.
The wedding dress in *Hello*
just couldn't be ignored.

When Debbie became Deborah
Cosmo did a feature on her car,
a gift from her dutiful husband.
A far cry from the Bigg Market
for Deborah rah rah rah.

Baz and the Mantle of Fidelity

Baz met Julie
at a party.
She was licking
jam from his navel
when he knew it was love

and her tongue
keeps him in place
to this day

happy watching
his tattoos
turn to fat,
gripping her hand
with his little band
of gold clinking
on his bitter.

Baz goes by
his Sunday name
these days,
works as a labourer.

Julie works
at the shirt factory,
gets reject shirts
for Christmas presents.

Baz loves Julie
and Julie loves Baz
it says so
on the sun visor
of their Ford Cortina.

Baz in the Garden of Eden

Baz has nicked
all the chicken wire
around the little forest
that grows near his estate.
'The kids brought a rabbit home!'
he explains,
has even swiped a couple of saplings
to stick in his back garden.

They look nice next to the geraniums
that he nicked off the council roundabout.

'They should plant more conifers…
our lass likes them' he adds,
snapping off oak for his dog to chase.

Julian and the Land of the Rising Sun

Julian is a kamikaze pilot.
He works on the buses.
The work is dangerous
a one way ticket and
no change given.
His passengers
are nervous,
gazing beyond the *No Smoking* signs,
communing with Nexus the god of public transport,
maybe today is the day they think
as half-remembered bus journeys flash past,
maybe today they will get their tickets punched,

watching the winding of the roll display
until the destination reaches *Oblivion.*

Julian is a kamikaze pilot
moving at breakneck speed towards
red lights, the spurred sun wrapped
around his forehead.
Gambling on the highway code
rule 1945
give way to buses driven by psychopaths

He narrows his eyes
at mushroom clouds in rear-view mirrors,

the woman with a bus pass
lip-reads his whispered '*Banzai*!'

Rising like dawn
from out of the pages of *The Sun*
a taxi driver who thinks he
is Biggles.

Endgame.

Baz 1891 and Cherry Red 1460

A desperate pleading phonecall,
tears caught in all that machismo.
'Come round, mate, please'.

Five minutes and several amber lights later
I hear the thud of *Symarip* cutting the suburbs.
It changes to *Prince Buster* as I cross the threshold.

After *Catch a Fire*
and a special segue into *The Specials*
I realise why I have been summoned.
Boots.
Standard Issue Black Dr. Martens and
Antiqued Cherry Red Classic 1460's piled on
a pyre in the backyard with
various monkey boots and
Major Dommo's.
He wants us to shave our heads.
I refuse.
He wants an airwair tattoo.
He settles for the Anaheim sound.

Flames lace the twelve holes.
We drink to Dr Funck and Dr. Martens
and Bill Griggs
and to battles lost and won.

It is the end of the world.

Baz Karaoke

'It means empty orchestra
but what does that mean?'

Baz stretches the term vocal stylist to its limits

honking through a tearful *My Way*
and bastard filing the edges off *I Will Survive*

dueting with Julie on *You're the One That I Want*,
a ghastly Travolta and a size 16 out of tune Sandy,
breathless in beer kissed moments

their kids hiding their faces
beneath hands suddenly too small.

'It means empty orchestra', Baz repeats
as if saying it twice will bring enlightenment.

Keeling over in the Labour club
like a diseased elm.

Baz Donne

In a world of air and angels
Baz at the end of his tether,
incapable of convalescence,
gasping at life and waiting
for the iron bishop to give
the last rites.
Bites back on the swirl
of the pipes that surround him
in a haze of ventolin he
reaches for his cigarettes.
Maybe he'll go out
in a blaze of glory,
blowing up the oxygen
taking some of these poor bastards
with him, but strength is failing
and his skin stretches over his bones
like gold to airy thinness
beaten and bowed, raises his eyes
to the clouds and skulking angels,
the last words of a devil,
whispered to
the prettiest nurse,

'Fucked….

Saint Baz

All this while
as he achieved sainthood
writing his own canon
a halo from bent wire
as in a school nativity;
tatty tinsel twined.

All this time
we hadn't noticed
his miracles;

the miracle of the broken nose,
the vision of the buttocked moon,
sticking 'Rolling Rocks' away
on Egyptian building sites.

A joiner following the family trade,
constructing Solomon's temple,
'I know all the handshakes'
he grins,
fluttering his hands
like Al Jolson

in the diaspora of those other saints
Wilson, Kepple and Betty.

Baz R.I.P.

At his funeral
no one said much
tasting the grim purgatory
of children sobbing.
Strange that we never
credited him with
being much of a Father.
'Barry' as the vicar eulogises
was many things to many people,
Father, husband, brother, son
but this list does not capture him.

If I was a betting man
I'd bet against God.
but I would love
to believe in Heaven
if only to see that daft get's face
pushed up against the Pearly Gates.

Die Young Stay Pretty
he once promised me
when we were young
and in love with Debbie Harry,
and his smile never dipped
when some monkeyhanger said,

'In order to die pretty you
can't be an ugly twat to start with.'

Acknowledgements

Some of these poems have appeared in the following books and magazines: *Public* (Iron Press), *Baz Poems* (Rebel Inc), *Red Sky at Night* (Five Leaves), *Hardly Literature*, *Moodswing*, *Star Trek: The Poems* (Iron Press), *The Yonkly*, *Views of Views*, *The Echo Room Yearbook* and *Heterosexual Honkies.*

Ta to Andy Willoughby at Hydrogen Jukebox
(ta for the music Matt!)

thanks to Kevin Williamson.

dedicated to every Baz I have known including myself

and to Crista Ermiya
for believing they were worth the effort.

for Dave, Tony, Alan, Barry, Big John, Stan, Linton, Paul, John, Kev and Peter because they know of what I speak.

For The Poetry Vandals, The Hardly Boys
and the 'Dirty Water' tribe.

Joanna Piesse, Kate Griffin, Kath Kenny ,
Angel Readman and Adam Fish

and to
Mr.Cooper, Mr Parkinson and Mr Barrass
the only teachers who ever made a difference.

Lastly to Shabnam, Matt, Shani and Charlie.